Great Than a Tourist – Venezuela

50 Travel Tips from a Local

> TOURIST

Author: Andrés Aguilera

Lock Haven, PA

ISBN: 9781521154656

DEDICATION

This book is dedicated to Venezuelans around the world: Stay proud and positive.

BOOK DESCRIPTION

Are you excited about planning your next trip?
Do you want to try something new while traveling?
Would you like some guidance from a local?

If you answered yes to any of these questions, then this book is just for you.

Greater than a Tourist Venezuela by Andrés Aguilera offers the inside scope.
Most travel books tell you how to travel like a tourist. Although there's nothing wrong with that, as a part of the Greater than a Tourist series this book will give you tips and a bunch of ideas from someone who lives at your next travel destination

In these pages you'll discover local advice that will help you throughout your stay. Greater than a tourist is a series of travel books written by locals. Travel like a local. Get the inside scope. Slow down, stay in one place, take your time, get to know the people and the culture of a place. Try some things off the beaten path with guidance. Patronize local business and vendors when you travel. Be willing to try something new and have the travel experience of a lifetime.

By the time you finish this book, you will be excited to travel to your next destination.

So grab YOUR copy today. You'll be glad you did.

INTRODUCTION

"The world is a book, and those who do not travel read only one page." –
Saint Augustine

As a born and raised Venezuelan, I was always surrounded by natural
beauty, color, mesmerizing views. However, as a little kid I did not
appreciate the breath taking quality of the landscapes I would run into, at
least not enough. I felt, somehow, apathetic and unaffected, to the point
where I even considered moving to a different continent.

When I grew older, I had the opportunity to travel my country from north
to south, east to west, an eye opening experience that would change the way
I saw Venezuela forever. I swam in the crystalline waters of Los Roques, I
played with the snow at the top of the Pico Bolívar, I contemplated the
majestic beauty of Canaima. All these places had a profound impact on my
life, inflicting a desire to speak up for my nation, to build a stronger pride
for my home.

I used to think that flying around the world would allow me to show some
gratitude for the people I got to know and the lands I explored during my
childhood. To my surprise, I didn't have to leave to find my voice; I didn't
need to spend months away from our national treasures or to miss my
loved ones to regain inspiration. This book is an open invitation you won't
be able to refuse, 50 reasons to meet my biggest muse to date: Venezuela.

Let me guide you through paradise in these pages.

CONTENTS

CONTENTS

Author Bio

WELCOME TO > TOURIST

1. Speak Venezuelan

5. Feel the Blues in Los Roques

6. Chill in Los Andes

7. Closer to Heaven

8. Hiking the Avila

9. Lightning Strikes

10. Temple of DUNES

11. Get a Tan in Margarita

12. Rum Tasting

13. Miss Venezuela

14. Let the Music Play

15. Our National Dish

16. In Case Of Doubt, Make Arepas

17. Chocolate

18. The world's largest oil reserves

19. Fly With Troupials

20. Smell The Flowers

21. Hit A Home Run

22. Score A Goal

23. Reverón's Paintings

24. It's All About Perspective

25. Soto's Simmetry

26. Our Lady Of Coromoto

27. The Divine Shepherdess

28. Marching On Carnival

29. Venezuelan Christmas

30. Cooking Hallacas

31. Keeping Up With The Gaitas

32. María Lionza

33. Our Currency

34. Sing The National Anthem

35. Party In Elorza

36. Dance With The Devil(s)

37. Uncle Simón's Blessing

38. When We Go to Maracaibo

39. Seasons

40. Virgin of Peace

41. One, Two, Three, Four

42. Coat of Arms

43. Yellow, Blue and Red

44. Chase the Sun

45. Simón Bolívar

46. The Largest Rodent in the World

47. Explore the Cave

48. Let the River flow

49. Drop the Caddle

50. Being Venezuelan

> TOURIST

Author Bio

Andrés is a twenty-something years old journalist with a passion (addiction?) to Social Media. He spends way too much on candies, updates his Itunes library on a daily basis and considers himself an unpaid foodie, which means he likes to eat. A lot.

 He enjoys roadtrips and meeting new places whenever he can, always with a perfectly-curated playlist. He's passions include: Writing, online shopping, languages, technology. You can follow him on Instagram as @aandress_ if you enjoy selfies, sunsets or photos of trees.

WELCOME TO > TOURIST

1. Speak Venezuelan

Let's start with the basics: We are the South American, Spanish speaking country who puts the "L" in "Loud" and "Latinos". Accents may vary in different regions of Venezuela, but for the most part we just talk really fast, passionately. There are slangs in our vocabulary that you probably would want to get familiar with, here's some examples:

- Chamo/Chama: Used to address boys (chamo) and girls (chama). In our language, this is the equivalent to "dude", "mate", etc. If someone refers to you using these words, there's a strong chance they are being friendly.

- Pana: This term could mean you're likeable or we consider you a friend, in a higher sense than just calling you a chamo/chama. We also use this one in plural to talk about and describe our group of friends.

- Vaina: The word with a million meanings! Everything is a *vaina* for us, so to make it short; you could compare this expression to "thing" or "stuff" in conversations. Brought up with both positive and negative connotations, this is a very popular term for Venezuelans everywhere.

- Epa: A short way to greet people, or to emphasize in discussions. When someone comes to you and say this, you may liken it to a simple "hey" in your head. On the other hand, if you hear it in a middle of a dialogue, view it as a method to highlight what's being said. Focus on the context.

 Other common words are "chévere" (similar to "cool"), "arrecho" or "arrecha" (used to talk about being incredibly mad or to refer to something impressing). We are a social, welcoming, warm nation, so don't be afraid to ask questions!

2. *Find Us*

As mentioned before, Venezuela is a South American country, specifically located at the northern extreme of South America. We share borders with Guyana to the east, Colombia to the west, Brazil to the south, and the Caribbean Sea to the North.

Meantime, our shoreline got some tropical neighbors to the north: Grenada, Barbados, Curaçao, Bonaire, Aruba, Saint Vincent, Trinidad and Tobago, and the Grenadines and the Leeward Antilles.

3. Meet Our Capital

Venezuela's capital is Caracas, a fast paced cosmopolitan city filled with music, colors and life.

There's always something to do in Caracas: You can party until the sun comes up in its night clubs, taste high quality gastronomy from all over the world, explore the Ávila (more on that later), and so much more!

You can move through the city using taxis, buses and the famous subway. However, with a population of around 4 million, I can assure you it's going to be crowded everywhere you go.

4. The World's Highest Waterfall

The Salto Ángel (or Angel Falls), one of our most popular touristic attractions, it's a part of Canaima National Park, located in the Gran Sabana of Bolivar state.

This breathtaking waterfall has a height of 3,212 feet (979 meters). To give you an idea of how tall it is, let's say at least 15 times bigger than the Niagara Falls and, by the time the water gets to the ground, it turns into fog.

 Fun fact: Disney's movie "Up" was largely inspired by The Gran Sabana and its tepuis (tabletop mountains like the Auyantepui, home to Angel Falls).

5. *Feel the Blues in Los Roques*

Another Venezuelan national park is Los Roques, an archipielago formed by 50 islands with crystalline waters and white sand.

To get to Los Roques, you need to take a flight from Caracas, Porlamar and Maracaibo, or you can find someone with a yacht. However, I would recommend you to buy planes ticket, so you can witness all the beautiful shades of blue from the air.

Once you're there, there's a great variety of things to do: From snorkeling, windsurfing and kite surfing, to exploring the keys and enjoying delicious sea food.

6. Chill in Los Andes

Even though we're a Caribbean country, you can also witness chilly landscapes and lower temperatures in Venezuela.

Los Andes are made of valleys, lagoons, mountains (some of them snowy) and small towns full of history. If relaxation is what you are looking for, this is the spot to visit.

On the other hand, Mérida City in Los Andes hosts one of the most important universities in Venezuela. Therefore, you can find a youthful spirit throughout the entire town which includes an active night life.

7. Closer to Heaven

Venezuela holds another record with the Mérida Cable Car system, the highest and second longest cable car in the world.

Using the cable car (named Mukumbarí) means a one of a kind journey of 12.5 kilometers up to Pico Espejo, or Mirror Peak, just across the Bolivar Peak, the highest point in our nation.

There are four stations you go through as the cable car keeps moving upwards; each of them displays the beauty of Mérida's mountains, valleys, lagoons and snow. This is a MUST if you decide to visit us.

8. Hiking the Avila

Referred by many as "the lung of Caracas", the Avila National Park it's a mountain full of activities for visitors such as hiking, excursions, cable car, and more.

As you climb, the views of Caracas and the fresh air will leave you speechless. Don't forget: Sporty clothes, water, and sweater.

9. Lightning Strikes

For those in the search for a unique, once in a lifetime experience, the Catatumbo Lightning is NOT to be missed.

This phenomenon happens in Lake Maracaibo, at the Zulia state, and holds the record for "highest concentration of lightning" in the world with an average of 28 lightning flashes per minute on a wet season.

Even if you're afraid of storms, watching the sky illuminate at night with such intensity it's an unforgettable sight. However, if you decide to see it, do it around October, at its peak.

10. Temple of DUNES

Adding another name to the list of unique places in the Venezuelan geography, Los Medanos (or Dunes) in Coro are THE spot to go to release your inner child.

 Located in the Falcón state, this small desert allows you to play with sand, running and rolling down a photo worthy landscape of hillsides.

 Just two things:

a) You may end up completely cover in sand, thanks to its normally windy weather.

 b) A sandcastle it's not going to last.

> TOURIST

"Traveling – it leaves you speechless, then turns you into a storyteller." –
Ibn Battuta

11. Get a Tan in Margarita

Margarita Island has a beach for every taste: With or without waves, crowded or isolated. Margarita is one of the most popular locations for tourist and it's only 25 minutes away from Caracas by plane, but you can also get there in a couple of hours by Ferry from Puerto La Cruz or Cumana, at Venezuela's west.

 Besides the beautiful beaches, the island offers you malls for shopping, spas and exclusive hotels for relaxation, horse riding, surf, windsurf, golf and a wild nightlife for party animals.

12. Rum Tasting

If you enjoy a drink every now and then, I highly recommend Venezuelan rum, one of two classes of rum in the world awarded with the Denomination of Origin Controlled (DOC) category for high quality standards.

Brands like Santa Teresa have established their dark and white rums on top on the liquor industry for their exquisite flavor. They also offer tasting sessions mixed with rugby games in their ranch, promoting team work and tradition.

13. Miss Venezuela

Beauty pageants are a national tradition, with Miss Venezuela in the spotlight.

For years, Venezuelan women had represented our country with dignity and won contests such as Miss Universe (seven titles), Miss World (six titles), Miss International (seven titles) and Miss Earth (two titles).

 As a consequence, Venezuelan women are considered among the most beautiful women in the world. Combining exotic features, confidence and hard work, they have made a name for themselves, to the point where we got two Miss Universe crowns in a row.

14. Let the Music Play

Music is a big part of a regular Venezuelan's life. We love to listen and dance to all kinds of Caribbean rhythms such as merengue, salsa and bachata.

However, the one that stands out the most it's our national dance: Joropo, a combination of harps, cuatros and maracas originated in the Llanos (or Plains).

15. Our National Dish

The biggest representation of Venezuelan cuisine it's the Pabellón, an extra tasty dish with black beans, white rice, fried fried plantains and shredded beef.

 Other versions of Pabellón can include avocado, white cheese or fried egg.

16. In Case Of Doubt, Make Arepas

Most Venezuelans eat arepas, at least, once a day. A very versatile meal, arepas are usually make for breakfast, but can also be a great dinner choice or a companion for lunch.

 Pretty much every Venezuelan family has its own way to make arepas, but to make it short they're rounded corn cakes that you can fry or grill. You can fill you arepa with any ingredient, but there's a couple of traditional ones to acknowledge:

a) Reina Pepiada: Meaning something similar to "beauty queen", this combination was born in 1955 to honor our first Miss World, Susana Duijm. It mixes avocado with mayonnaise, shredded chicken, cilantro and lime.

b) Sifrina: Add a bit of shredded cheese to the Reina Pepiada to get this kind of arepa, for the "preppy snobs"

c) Dominó: Named after dominoes (a regular game in the llanos of Venezuela), this kind of arepa also includes black and ingredients such as hard cheese and black beans.

d) Pelúa: Meaning "hairy" in Spanish, pulled beef and shredded cheese get together to form a very delicious kind of arepa.

e) Catira: Shredded yellow cheese + Pieces of shredded chicken = the blonde arepa.

17. Chocolate

Venezuelan cacao is considered "the most flavorful and aromatic in the world" among experts.

With a sweeter taste than other countries', our cacao beans are renowned for their high quality.

Chuao, a village at the central coast of Venezuela, has become a recurrent stop for chocolate gourmets. There, you can see cacao plants on your way to the beach and taste its fruit before its turned into delicious bars and bonbons.

18. The world's largest oil reserves

Yes, another record. Venezuela has almost 300 billion oil barrels in reserves, the world's largest to date.

A big part of our economy relies on oil exportations, but we also have the eighth largest proven natural gas reserves (around 21,000 quadrillion cubic feet).

As a result, we enjoy the cheapest petrol on a global scale, which makes it easier to take road trips.

19. Fly With Troupials

Our national bird it's the Venezuelan Troupial (Icterus icterus), a representation of the troupial species with shades of orange, yellow, black and white.

This bird can be spotted in dry areas like plains, where they live on a diet made out of eggs, insects, fruit and small birds.

20. Smell The Flowers

When it comes to flowers, Venezuela is known for its orchids, specially our national emblematic one: Cattleya mossiae(commonly named "Flor de Mayo" or "May Flower").

This gorgeous flower fully blossoms in spring time with an incredible color scheme made out of different shades of purple. During the season, Cattleyas release a hypnotic perfume that no words can describe accurately.

"Man cannot discover new oceans unless he has the courage to lose sight of the shore." – Andre Gide

21. Hit A Home Run

An American sport that has become a part of Venezuelan culture, baseball games have the biggest attendance numbers in our country.

There's even a rivalry almost equal to Montagues and Capulets in Romeo and Juliet: Leones del Caracas (Caracas' Lions, our capital's team) vs. Navegantes Del Magallanes (Magallanes' Navigators, from the Carababo state).

From October to January, you can feel the euphoria in our baseball fields, or in the majority of Venezuelan homes through TV. Baseball it's more than just a hobby for us, it is a lifestyle!

22. Score A Goal

Futbol (football, how we call soccer) it's another beloved sport for Venezuelans.

 Not only do we worship our national team, La Vinotinto (The Burgundy), we got nothing but love for our states' teams, we watch every world cup, even when La Vinotinto it's not assisting, and we follow European leagues religiously.

23. Reverón's Paintings

When it comes to Venezuelan art, Armando Reverón comes to mind. He was a painter and sculptor notorious for his use of natural elements to paint, his oceanic inspiration for color and lights, as well as his dolls and women portraits.

 Reverón remains an influence in impressionism for artists because of his achievements during the 19th century.

24. It's All About Perspective

A specialist in kinetic art, Carlos Cruz-Diez has made a name for himself in galleries worldwide.

This Venezuelan pioneer's signature is a mixture of color, lines and perspective. His work involves the viewer, changing according to perception.

You can see his signature lineal composition in the streets of Venezuelan, even on the floor tiles of our International Airport, a popular spot for photos.

25. Soto's Simmetry

There are showcases of Jesús Soto's art near every corner of Caracas. Remembered for his use of flat colors, symmetry and geometric forms, Soto's sculptures and minimalistic paintings have been exhibited (and appreciated) internationally.

26. Our Lady Of Coromoto

Like the majority of latin countrys, we are, for the most part, a catholic nation.

In that sense, it's impossible not to talk about Our Lady Of Coromoto, Patroness of Venezuela.

 She's believed to be an apparition of Virgin Mary who showed up in Guanare, a small town in the plains of our country, in 1652. A sanctuary for the Virgin of Coromoto was built in Guanare and declared a minor basilica by Pope Benedict XVI.

27. The Divine Shepherdess

Another significant religious figure for Venezuelans it's the Divine Shepherdess from Barquisimeto, in the Lara state.

She's believed to represent Virgin Mary too, holding a baby Jesus with a lamb next to her. Her importance it's proven with a procession devoted to her every January 14, when thousands of citizens from the entire country follow the statue around the Barquisimeto streets.

Said procession is thought to be one of the most prominent in the world.

28. Marching On Carnival

Time to talk about Venezuelan holidays, starting with an extremely colorful one: Carnival

We get two free days to celebrate carnival, which says a lot of how big this festivity is. During those days you can watch or participate in parades (depending of the city you visit) with striking allegoric cars, tons of confetti, marching bands and lots of dancing.

Small towns got another tradition: Filling small balloons with water to throw them at people. So, if you choose to go for a walk, watch out!

29. Venezuelan Christmas

Christmas in Venezuela it's a big deal. Families organize big feasts with hallacas (I'll get to that later), ham, salad, eggnog, music, etc.

On Christmas AND new years' eve, we like to dress up (preferably with brand new outfits), we take photos and engage in all kinds of silly, superstitious rituals like walking with suitcases to attract traveling, eating 12 grapes to grant 12 wishes and so much more.

On the other hand, instead of Santa Claus, Venezuelan kids wait for baby Jesus to drop presents underneath the Christmas tree.

30. Cooking Hallacas

Hallacas are a HUGE component of Venezuelan Christmas. Every year, families gather together to prepare these tasty dishes while they listen to some gaitas (I'll elaborate on that next).

To keep it short, an hallaca it's made out of corn dough and filled with meat, chicken, pork and, sometimes, all of the above.

Other ingredients include green olives, raisins and annatto oil to color the corn dough.

After they're done, hallacas are wrapped inside plantain or banana leaves and refrigerated. Most families end up eating all the way up to January.

> TOURIST

"Adventure is worthwhile." – Aesop

31. Keeping Up With The Gaitas

No Venezuelan Christmas is complete without gaitas, a type of folk music from the Zulia state.

The themes for gaitas include happiness, humor, protest, romance and nostalgia. They're mostly played through December, both live and on the radio, but in some parts of the country you can start to hear them on September or even August.

Instruments for gaitas include the furro, maracas, cuatro, charrasca and tambora (a kind of drum invented in Venezuela). To keep it simple, think of gaitas as our own Christmas Carol.

32. María Lionza

An icon to alternative religions in Venezuela, María Lionza is the main figure for a religion that blends Catholicism, African and Indigenous beliefs, compared to the santería.

She's represented as a powerful woman on top of a Tapir what appears to be a female pelvis, as a token of fertility. A mountain called Sorte in the Yaracuy State it's used to worship María Lionza with all kinds of tribal dances and offerings.

33. Our Currency

The Bolívar or Bolívar Fuerte, named after our Liberator, Simón Bolívar, was adopted as Venezuela's currency in 1879.

Venezuela's Bolívar is symbolized as "Bs.F" or "Bs" and its nicknames are "bolo", "real" and "luca" (at least for now).

34. Sing The National Anthem

A melody that represents pride and hope, the "Gloria Al Bravo Pueblo" (glory to the brave people) has remained our national anthem since 1881.

With lyrics by Vicente Salias and music by José Landaeta, we know this song by heart and sing it respectfully in school, sport events and more.

35. Party In Elorza

Elorza it's a Venezuelan town located in the Apure state, part of our beautiful plains.

On March 29 of every year, the Fiesta en Elorza (Party In Elorza) gathers people from all sides of the country to enjoy llaneras and folk music, dance joropo, ride horses and, overall, celebrate and honor San José (St. Joseph).

This party usually includes coleo (stay tuned to read more about it), beauty pageants to pick the queen of this festivity and sporty competitions.

36. Dance With The Devil(s)

It's time to talk about of Venezuela's most unique traditions and holydays: The Dancing Devils of Corpus Christi.

Recognized by UNESCO for its cultural heritage, this holiday finds men, women and even children dressed as red devils with colorful masks dancing to represent the God's victory over the devil, good defeating evil.

Though the festivity spread across the country, Diablos de Yare (Devils of Yare) in Miranda State are most notorious, reuniting nine Thursdays after Holy Thursday to parade around San Francisco de Yare's main square.

37. Uncle Simón's Blessing

Simón Díaz, called "tío Simón" o uncle Simón by older Venezuelans, was one of our country's most notorious musicians, awarded with several Grammy awards for his folk compositions.

His songs have been covered by musicians such as Gypsy Kings, Celia Cruz, Julio Iglesias, Juan Gabriel, Plácido Domingo, and many others.

"Caballo Viejo" (old horse), his biggest song, was inspired by the beauty of Venezuela's plains and their diversity, like the majority of his compositions.

Díaz died in 2014, but remains to this day one of our most influential artists.

38. *When We Go to Maracaibo*

Lake Maracaibo, in Zulia state, holds more than the already impressive Catatumbo Lightning. Not only is it one of the oldest lakes on Earth with around 37 MILLION years old, this lake's also one of the largest in the world with 13,210.

 Though it's not recommended to swim in its waters because of chemicals and contamination, one can't help to be mesmerized by its majestic presence when crossing the bridge that goes over it, the inspiration for a famous Venezuelan gaita: "Cuando Voy A Maracaibo" (when I go to Maracaibo).

39. Seasons

Let's keep this short and sweet: There's only two seasons in Venezuela.

Rainy (refer to as "winter" by some) normally lasts from May to November with Dry season ("summer") covering the rest of the year.

40. Virgin of Peace

State Trujillo, a part of the Andes region, it's to another religious icon for Venezuelans: Virgen de la Paz (Virgin of Peace).

This catholic image represents Virgin Mary and can be spotted in the city of Trujillo by far, with a 153-foot (46.72m) statue remaining Latin America's tallest monument.

> TOURIST

"Travel makes one modest. You see what a tiny place you occupy in the world." – Gustave Flaubert

41. One, Two, Three, Four

Four may be Venezuela's lucky number thanks to the Cuatro ("four" in Spanish), our traditional musical instrument.

Venezuelan Cuatros has four strings (hence the name), looks similar to a ukulele and was inspired by a four-string Spanish guitar that no longer exists.

It's sound it's magical and has given shape to folklore or Venezuela's folk music, llaneras and most of our music-related traditions.

42. Coat of Arms

Venezuela's Coat of Arms combines the following elements:

A) Wheat: A representation of wealth and union throughout the 20 states that existed when the Coat of Arms was created.

B) Three kinds of weapons: A sable, three lances and a sword tied up by two national flags to represent victory.

C) A white horse: Believed to symbolize freedom and inspired by Simón Bolivar's own horse "Palomo"

43. Yellow, Blue and Red

Our flag has gone through several versions, but the current one was introduced in 2006 based on the design for 1811's flag.

It has three stripes: The one on top in yellow represents the wealth and gold found in our country; the middle stripe it's blue to refer to the seas and shores, and the red stripe underneath has to do with the blood spilled to gain Venezuela's independence.

There's also a set of eight stars (they were seven in the original design) to represent provinces of Venezuela during the declaration of independence.

44. Chase the Sun

At the northwest of Venezuela, specifically in the Falcón state, you can come across another representation of Venezuela's natural beauty: Morrocoy National Park.

 Named after our own nickname for the Chelonoidis carbonaria (a red-footed tortoise), Morrocoy has a set of beautiful beaches with tons of sea species and corals.

 The park has a number of keys or small islands that you can visit through boat, all with crystalline waters, exotic birds and delicious sea food.

45. Simón Bolívar

A big figure in Venezuela's history, Simón Bolívar had a leader role when it came down to free Venezuela from Spanish rulers.

Among the nations that became sovereign states after Bolívar's troupes triumphed over the Spanish monarchy are Colombia, Perú, Ecuador, Bolivia, Panamá and Venezuela. He received the title of Liberator of Venezuela since.

Fun fact: His name is a mouthful, Simón José Antonio de la Santísima Trinidad Bolívar y Palacios. We all had to learn it in school.

46. The Largest Rodent in the World

Capybara (called chigüire in Venezuela) can be found in several South American countries, including ours.

 With looks that resemble guinea pigs, these mammals live in lakes and rivers located in the plains. They're red haired herbivores who live from eight to ten years.

They can reach 134 cm (3.48 to 4.40 ft) in length, and weigh from 35 to 66 kg (77 to 146 lb) as adults, making them the biggest rodent in the entire world.

47. Explore the Cave

In the Monagas state, at the northeastern part of the country, you can visit the Guácharo Cave National Park, a cavern longer than ten kilometers (six miles).

This cave was named after oilbirds (guácharos - Steatornis caripensis, species that can be seen flying across the whole cavern among 366 other kinds of birds.

Fun activities include bird watching, swimming in the Salto La Paila pools (20 minutes away from the cave), hiking and trekking.

48. Let the River flow

Orinoco River it's a part of the Amazonas state in Venezuela. This river is one of the longest in South America with 2,140 kilometers that flow between Colombia and Venezuela.

 Among the species living in the river, giant river otters, crocodiles and piranhas can be spotted from the tributaries (main transportation system across the Orinoco).

 When it comes to recreational activities, every April there's swimming contests with a large number of competitors.

49. Drop the Caddle

Coleo it's the Venezuelan equivalent to American rodeo.

This traditional sport consists of llaneros (cowboys) riding horses at full at full speed to catch cattle by the tail and then make it stumble. Whoever accomplishes this in the shortest amount of time, wins.

Coleo's popularity it's bigger in the plains, where men (and some women) start training at a very young age in mangas de coleo (spaces designed for its practice).

50. Being Venezuelan

Last but not least, I would like to put into words what being a Venezuelan means.

Venezuelan is synonym for having a sense of humor in every circumstance, laughing at yourself, at everyone around you, at life!

Being Venezuelans it's adapting to change and finding opportunities, open doors (sometimes even windows) at difficult times.

Venezuela's name may come from the Italian word "Veneziola" (meaning little Venice) but there's nothing more Latin, warm and unique than our country.

Venezuela equals diversity and I assure you, you will find a lot of things to look at, love and learn from when you visit us.

> TOURIST

> TOURIST

Greater than a Tourist

Please read other Greater than a Tourist Books.

Join the >Tourist Mailing List :
http://eepurl.com/cxspyf

Facebook:
https://www.facebook.com/GreaterThanATourist

Please leave your honest review of this book on Amazon and Goodreads. Thank you.

Printed in Poland
by Amazon Fulfillment
Poland Sp. z o.o., Wrocław